Some

Pink

Star

Sophie Essex

Some Pink Star
by Sophie Essex
ISBN: 978-1-908125-74-3

Cover Art by David Rix

Publication Date: March 2019

Eibon ale
Press

Several of these poems appeared previously at or within the following journals: *Burning House Press, HVTN, Lighthouse, Zarf*

For Felix

Contents

Titian Blue

talk of last night's halves
how close we came

our ripeness of air
       scorched violent

to *stultify*

to fuck then destroy each version of her

Periaqueductal Gray

reflexive   like *to calve*

(outside definitions)

       how my own balled-
       milky-fluth renders

       make me conceptual

I love the feeling when you say

       don't

IKB

I want scope for desire
         visible depth

she urgent
in immaculate summer heat

         too soon

each fist a readjustment

Vanilla Sky

because this is how you like it

Violet Volcanoes

distance is inevitably
          anti sound

luxurious *de*formation

.

Isabelline

domesticated

pitch of memory
palm-sized   muscle memory

tectonic in each seeded stroke

speak nothing new

an empire
jawline

unstable points of contact

un-   come

instigate our above sea level activity

Bubblegum

come   to know my mouth intimately
pearlised cleave of feminine consequence

baby how tender
          how woozy we are

barely noon and tired now of
          docile love

as content as body   as machine
                    as resource

baby how woozy I am

baby   come soft spit viability
          into the girl of me

Neutral Atmosphere

gentle collision   to begin with
languid multi-layered epic disintegration

off-white

the body of a woman cosseted assentive is
          unsteady to begin with

convulsive easy terror   /   a given

          love   to begin with

Icterine

consider my sensitivity to light
in relation to the colour of your support

an acceptable bruise   softening
& pleasure hiccups   sugaring

     a sudden loss of oxygen

how many possible accusations
how far can you go

     throat tight   pin-stuck
     I'm easily led

Cotton Candy

I choose to pay with my body uncoming
mistake participatory action for a threat

I'm into   possibilities
I'm into   situations

this skyline curves a fresh pink brutality
my nose   bleeds

　　　　we could do so much

& the same body arcs
in another direction

　　　　　　away from the soft geometric shapes
　　　　　　mouthed into me

I mewl like the young
sunlit & scorched & contradictory

in and out of

Atomic Number 78

eight tetrahedral voids sounds dreamy when you
    linger over an idea of us

    beg me to stay a while

    to endure
all your assumed anticipation

        shared rapturous flirtatious
            girl-on-girl
            riotous unease

        soft shifting acidic mucosa
            of possible future lovers

a heads-up:

I exist in greater abundance on the moon
    // am a landscape of oncoming promised velocity

corrupted common little silver pussy

This Is The Colour Of My Dreams

I drool pretty

>   slow choke on a promise of summer
>   infinite error

infinite   sawtoothing love into tenderness withheld

auto :: erotic

an easy creature bathed in lilac light

>   kitten
>   bunny
>   baby

fucked
each way

Sgr A*

tongue the upper parts
whilst I harvest desire

speak easy about gravity&
how you'll bring me down
    the weight of force   as consequence

the intrigue of kittens

the way trouble finds a girl
        not entirely accidental

how I'll cease to be a singular body

a body of evidence
    sweet & glorious little !   ))

so simple to shatter

I'll swallow a billion suns
    full & froth & oscillate
    I thought I thought I

Clove Pink

as if I avoid the sound men make when challenged

sea urchin in bathwater
needles of war
        parts placed out of reach
        etcetera

pre-   sleep & possess   cum &
        menstrual

kitten, that feels so
        brief   habitual affectionate

in order to desire :: objectify / capsize

        fill me up
        all curve   all bed of carnations

the potential of my pussy keeps you hard until

Silent Red Avalanche

& then   the damp glitter of resistance

fuck being too harsh-a-word for what this could be &
ought to be

keening tigress
        I come with the snow
        bloom like spilt milk

Pink Grapefruit

& we let it happen

snowmelt, an absence of asking
            excess of superficial wounds
/ cat-o-nine & clear ice

            our bodies lit polychromatic
pink hued with primal seduction
            exhausted by daylight

a mouthful   a reassurance

            those fuckable rabbits sprawled in
                    sensuous fever
                    saturated wide-eyed

how perfectly adapted we have become

Prickly Pear

at this hour lilac disruption comes with the knee
arousal teases ferocity
        & I'm overflowing

drunk little velvet lamb
un-   characteristically careless

surrendering all for the afterglow

and you   quiet other

I want you to say you love   *maybe*
maybe toy with me further

call me *a mouthful*   again
let me loose

come prove yourself also

lx

I too am relatively small
        a finely sculptured playfully amorous fucktoy

craving obelisk
the crook of his elbow   breath

        rosy pink rosy red
contusions razoring my curves gorgeously tender

I think about length
how geologic I must taste
      saltwater   the opposite of luxury

how I am an object only when I objectify myself

Cyanotic (a buried sounding)

I'm feeling that approaching air
soft sediment of bodily discharge
        blue of contrast

limbs arcuate
      appropriatcly
             under pressure

     how careless you are lover

lover I   am prone to saying no when
          no one is around
          am inclined to

in this absence
become

achingly knowingly
      vulnerable
      beneath

Honeysuckle

Say so much teeth makes a girl carnivorous
indispensable essential   several kinds of fantasy

       how sugar dissolves in water
       as compensation

violence must be excessive & precise
mutual terror   or threat

thick curvature of self

thumb tucked into palm   *provocative*

Yellowthroat

with the sun love is

      insinuation   rabid   distant
          a petty autumnal mechanism

I objectify the length of string gone missing
possess a natural history

swarm

side up-down I am deep throated splitting light
      a real girl retching up a good time

clotted oral   claggy

Pandarah

in a dream I have of you   I am pinned by a tiger
in a dream I have of you   tiger   bite

I mean oral / non-verbal

pelt of girl identical to other
        in such unreliable light

apex predation

bairn born without teeth

strange wounds

     hey kitty-kat   *hi!*

in a dream I have of you   I am unresponsive
guts spill like   guts spilling

    semi-sexual

Mechanical Fawn

three quarters of the way up

       spring swaddled plump white

tight bind

something she said

Snowfield

retreat.
bear my own weight.
take summer.   restrained.

          my mass. cubic metered
my heart. in santiago. cityscaped.
          makes you seem so shatteringly typical
a safe. space.

          snowfall equals. snowmelt.

what's happening where you are?

I take a slow crawl downward.
          leave you for a lifetime.   terminal.